Acclaim for

The 11 Questions All Donors Ask And the Answers All Donors Crave

"People often ask me which book they should read first to learn about fundraising. Now I've got an easy answer: Harvey McKinnon's *The 11 Questions Every Donor Asks*. I can't think of any other piece of writing in the fundraising field that packs so much insight into so few pages."

Mal Warwick, Author
Raising Thousand Dollar Gifts by Mail

"*The 11 Questions* contains straightforward, practical advice that ALL fundraisers should know. I have encountered these questions throughout my fundraising career and only wish I had Harvey's insight earlier; it would have made certain situations a lot easier!"

Paulette V. Maehara, President and CEO
Association of Fundraising Professionals (AFP)

"Ask the right questions and listen to and learn from your donors. Support for your cause will follow."

Tim Seiler, Director
The Fund Raising School and Public Service
The Center on Philanthropy at Indiana University

"The really crucial question is how quickly can you get a hold of this book and absorb its wisdom, so that you too will know what's in your donors' minds."

Ken Burnett, Author
Relationship Fundraising and *Friends for Life*

"In the time it takes to enjoy a leisurely meal, you can feast on the expert and inspiring advice of *The 11 Questions*. Peppered with engaging stories and seasoned with Harvey's light humor, this book will leave you fully satisfied!"

Rosemary Oliver, Director of Development
Amnesty International, Canad⌐

D0188890

Companion Books to *The 11 Questions*

Fund Raising Realities Every Board Member Must Face

A 1-Hour Crash Course on Raising Major Gifts for Nonprofit Organizations

David Lansdowne

If every board member of every nonprofit organization across America read this book, it's no exaggeration to say that millions upon millions of additional dollars would be raised.

How could it be otherwise when, after spending just *one* hour with this gem, board members everywhere would understand virtually everything they need to know about raising major gifts.

David Lansdowne distills the essence of major gifts fundraising, puts it in the context of 47 "realities," and delivers it all in unfailingly clear prose.

Among the *Top Three* bestselling fundraising books of all time.

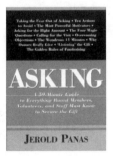

ASKING

A 59-Minute Guide to Everything Board Members, Volunteers, and Staff Must Know to Secure the Gift

Jerold Panas

It ranks right up there with public speaking. Nearly all of us fear it. And yet it's critical to the success of our organizations. Asking for money. It makes even the stout-hearted quiver.

But now comes a book, *Asking,* and short of a medical elixir, it's the next best thing for emboldening board members, volunteers, and staff to ask with skill, finesse … and powerful results.

What *Asking* convincingly shows is that it doesn't take stellar sales skills to be an effective asker. Nearly everyone, regardless of their persuasive ability, can become an effective fundraiser if they follow Panas' step-by-step guidelines.

Emerson & Church, Publishers
www.emersonandchurch.com

THE 11 QUESTIONS EVERY DONOR ASKS

AND THE ANSWERS ALL DONORS CRAVE

First printed June 2008

10 9 8 7 6 5 4 3 2 1

Printed in the United States of America

This text is printed on acid-free, FSC certified paper.

Emerson & Church, Publishers
P.O. Box 338 • Medfield, MA 02052
Tel. 508-359-0019 • Fax 508-359-2703
www.emersonandchurch.com

Library of Congress Cataloging-in-Publication Data

McKinnon, Harvey.
  The 11 questions every donor asks and the answers all
donors crave : how you can inspire someone to give
generously / by Harvey McKinnon.
     p. cm.
  ISBN 1-889102-37-7 (pbk. : alk. paper)
  1. Charities. 2. Charitable contributions. 3. Deferred
giving. 4. Charitable uses, trusts, and foundations. I. Title.
II. Title: Eleven questions every donor asks and the answers
all donors crave.
  HV40.M14 2008
  658.15'224—dc22

                                          2008018407

Foreword by Jerold Panas

THE 11 QUESTIONS
EVERY DONOR ASKS

AND THE ANSWERS ALL DONORS CRAVE

*How You Can Inspire Someone
To Give Generously*

HARVEY MCKINNON

Emerson
& Church
PUBLISHERS

To Marcia, James and Ian

FOREWORD

When I first heard about it, I thought – this is a book I've got to get my hands on. Right away.

Just imagine. Being able to identify the very questions donors are most likely to ask before making their gift. Being able to pin those down would be enlightening. Isn't that what every fundraiser and volunteer wants to know in advance of making a call?

I'm not shy, so I called the Publisher to ask if I could get my hands on an advance copy of the book. I didn't want to wait till it was printed. I said I'd settle for a typed manuscript. And that's what they sent me. Edit marks and all.

I didn't want to wait because, darn it, I had some calls to make. And if I could find some important tips, I wanted to know about them. I need all the help I can get. Everyone does, no matter how experienced you are.

What I uncovered is a treasure chest.

The author delivers on his promise. What Harvey McKinnon gives us are 11 of the most penetrating questions donors will ask you. And if they don't actually ask them, it's what they're thinking. You can count on it.

That's precisely why you need to be prepared. Leaving just one of these questions unanswered can trip you up in securing the gift.

It all seems so obvious now. I wonder why I hadn't made a list of these myself. And, curiously, there aren't 10 questions. And there aren't 12. I tried to think of another major question and I can't. The author has identified them all.

Harvey McKinnon is a veteran fundraiser and a marvelous wordsmith. He's produced a beautifully polished gem, with real-life stories that unerringly hit their mark, like an arrow piercing the center of a bulls-eye.

Wait till you read about the postage stamp and why it took 25 years to get the gift. Bingo! It all comes alive, like Harvey's response to the person who said: "Will you leave my office right now if I give you a check for $1,000?"

Perhaps I like *The 11 Questions* so much because I agree with Harvey on every point. (Hey, what can I say? Two great minds ... and all that stuff.) I suggest you dive headlong into this book, which is certain to become a classic.

They say a donor's objections are your best

friends. Well, they're not, not if you don't know the questions and, of course, the answers. So get ready for a lively adventure into the mind of a donor. You've got the best tour guide I could imagine.

Jerold Panas

Jerold Panas

INTRODUCTION

A child going to a new school wonders: Will the other children like me? Will the teacher be nice? Will I make friends?

A teenager wonders: Am I attractive? Can I get tickets to the concert? Can I afford that new jacket?

A new parent wonders: Will my child be healthy? Will she be successful in life? Will I ever sleep through the night again?

A potential donor wonders: How much can I give? Do I really care enough about this cause? Will my gift have an impact?

These questions – and thousands more like them – run through our brains continually. Most don't even reach a conscious level.

To succeed at fundraising, it's essential to know <u>the</u> questions that are on your donor's mind. And the better you are at answering those questions, the more money you're certain to raise.

This book poses the 11 critical questions.

As you know, our minds aren't just logical tools helping us to function everyday. They're complex emotional and chemical soups, governed by nature and nurture. Everyone has a daily diet of "Should I?" "Can I?" "What if?" "Will they?" "When?" – questions whose answers determine our actions and, in some cases, our future. This is how our minds work. And it's also how the brains of our donors operate.

The rich are no different from you or me, except they have more money and better teeth. Probably better holidays too. But essentially they're the same. They constantly ask themselves questions too.

And tapping into their thoughts and feelings will equip you with the best responses to their questions.

To write this book I drew on my three decades of fundraising for a wide variety of causes, large and small, from global brands to start-ups. I've worked in many countries and taught fundraising in many more. I interviewed both fundraisers and major donors. And I called on a lot of friends for their best stories.

But enough of that. You've got money to raise. So let's get to the questions.

–HM

CONTENTS

THE QUESTIONS

1

"Why Me?"

If you have teenagers (or have been one), you know the person the world revolves around.

Or if by some quirk of nature your kids are model cherubs, think back to that blind date. "Enough about me," your companion said. "Let's talk about you. What do *you* think about me?"

Or, perhaps it's an elderly neighbor you recall. You asked with civility, "How are you?" only to be subjected to a list of ailments spanning their entire anatomy.

"Me" is everyone's favorite subject.

So it's no surprise that a donor's first question (whether spoken or not) is ... Why me? And it's a loaded question.

By asking it, the donor is trying to situate himself in the world, or at least in *your* world. Going through his mind – simultaneously –are related concerns: How do you see me? Do I approve of the way you see me? Do you really know me? Do you care about me? Am I important to you for reasons other than my money?

Carol is someone who had such questions.

After a distinguished career in public health, she retired and devoted herself to a number of organizations serving seniors. Noted author and consultant, Mal Warwick, who at the time was establishing a community foundation focused on young people, approached Carol and asked if she'd become a Founder. His goal: a gift of $5,000.

"Why me?" she asked. "You know I never give more than $1,000 at a time. And my interest is seniors, not youth. Why should I do this?"

This is a common dilemma fundraisers face. Virtually all people predisposed to philanthropy are already donors to some causes. It can be tough to break into their "circle of concern." And yet it is possible, as you'll see in Mal's case.

"Knowing she was fully capable of giving $5,000, and that she viewed herself as a community leader, I felt I could persuade her to join the Founders group," says Mal. "The challenge was to relate our mission to her fondest interests. So I asked whether she saw any contradiction in helping young people rather than seniors.

Mal is nothing if not astute.

"The question caught her off guard," he continues. "She started thinking out loud about intergenerational programs in which young people help seniors with household chores while the seniors, in turn, mentor the young.

"She recalled the young people who had joined in a program she herself was running. As she spoke at length about this intergenerational concept – novel at the time – she talked herself into giving the $5,000. The amount wasn't the problem. All she needed was an excuse to give."

Mal knew exactly what he was doing. In a kind and respectful way he allowed Carol to discover that she also cared about their community's youth. Like most people, she wanted to help. And by posing that one perfect question, Mal solved her problem of priorities, and Carol became a Founder.

As this example shows, the art of fundraising is the ability to help donors understand how your cause meshes with their personal interests and how, by entrusting you with their money, they'll achieve something they want: namely, improving the lives of others.

The "Why me?" question can also be answered with:

• Because with your past gifts you've shown you care.

• Because you've met so and so (a person the cause

has helped) and your gift can help others like her.

• Because you're respected and your support will inspire others.

• Because you know how big the need is, and your gift will help provide solutions.

There are many other answers, of course. You'll identify the best one by deepening your understanding of the donor.

■ Involving donors emotionally.

In most campaigns, the bulk of gifts will come from your current donors. They're the ones who have already demonstrated their concern and commitment. However, there are other good prospects, often community leaders, who haven't given to you. When you approach these individuals, they'll almost certainly be asking "Why me?"

Jimmie Alford is one of America's great fundraisers. Let's see how he coached a volunteer to respond to this question.

The organization in question focused on mental health. It had virtually no donor base and no fundraising experience. What was sorely needed were prospects with giving capacity *and* leadership qualities. Jimmie, with some help from the board, identified such a person: a respected community leader – let's call her Sue – who also had the means to make a major gift.

Jimmie's volunteer called for an appointment.

Without hesitation, Sue tried to put her off, saying she wasn't likely to make a gift. "We're not asking you for a gift," the volunteer quickly replied. "We want something as helpful – your advice."

Sue agreed to meet. And at their meeting the volunteer shared with her a number of success stories related to mental health. She also talked about specific individuals whose lives had been transformed by the organization. Sue understood and related. Like many of us she'd been touched by mental health issues in her family. She offered lots of advice and more than a few contacts.

The volunteer didn't ask for a gift but did request a follow-up meeting to report on how she was doing as a result of Sue's advice. The following week Sue sent a check for $2,500.

Thirty days later the volunteer visited Sue a second time. Again, she didn't ask for a gift, but shared the progress she was making based on Sue's input. Again, the volunteer made only one request: could she report back and seek Sue's advice again in 30 days?

One week later a second check, this time for $25,000, arrived at the organization's door.

After the third visit, Sue was heavily involved emotionally. For her, the volunteer and the organization she represented, had become the face for mental health issues. Again, even though she wasn't asked, Sue sent a third check within days. This time for $150,000 to honor her husband who had died the year before.

Touched by the impact the organization was making, and knowing she could help financially, Sue had answered the question "Why me?" for herself.

2

"Why Are *You* Asking Me?"

My uncle Russell once said to his wife Annie, "You must admit men have better judgment than women." Annie replied, "That's certainly true. You married me, and I married you."

Whether women have better judgment isn't a discussion I'll entertain in these pages. For that, wait for my next book, *Putting Your Foot in It*.

But one thing I do know is this. The first thing prospects judge, even before your proposal or your cause, is Y-O-U.

They take your full measure, which typically means any or all of the following:

- "Who are you?"
- "What's in it for you?"

- "Have *you* given?"
- "Who else has given?" And,
- "Do *you* genuinely believe in this cause?"

■ Who are you?

A friend? A peer? A stranger? Are you volunteer or staff? All things being equal, the closer your connection to the prospect, the better your odds are of obtaining a gift.

Sure, at times it's easier for a friend to say no, but my experience (and that of many fundraisers) is that it's painfully hard to turn away a close acquaintance who's passionate about a good cause. Too much is at stake emotionally.

Besides friendship, what else helps? Titles. An organization's CEO will open more doors (and wallets) than an Assistant Manager for Small Dollar Gifts. Unfair, perhaps, but undeniable. The fact that your campaign chair or board president is asking underscores the importance of the gift.

Also, local or national standing play a role. A highly respected community leader or an Olympic medalist will open doors – and checkbooks as well.

Then there's the matter of business relationships. If the person asking is in a position to benefit your company or your career, she's harder to refuse.

Lastly, if the solicitor is someone known for impeccable integrity, (think Nelson Mandela or a similar personage in your sphere), then the chances for success are measurably increased.

■ What's in it for you?

When a donor thinks, "What's your particular interest in asking me for money," the underlying question is: What are your motives? And motives mean everything.

If the person you're asking feels you're sacrificing your time for the cause, that your passion is genuine, and that you truly care how the gift will be used, then the question, "What's in it for you?" will be laid to rest.

If on the other hand donors feel you're deriving some personal benefit, they're less likely to be interested.

David Dunlop, one of the co-creators of Moves Management™ and a truly great fundraiser, sums it up this way: "If we are really skillful in our work, we'll have people asking who are so deeply committed to our cause that the answer to why are *you* asking is obvious."

A worthy goal indeed.

■ Have *you* given?

One of the first lessons I learned in fundraising is that it's difficult to ask if you haven't given yourself.

Imagine if a donor asks the solicitor: "What have

you given?"

Does the solicitor inspire a gift by replying, "Hey, I'm giving my time – that's *my* gift."

Because that's when the would-be donor stows his wallet and says – "Then sign me up for a few hours Saturday morning."

There are no inspiring or successful answers if you haven't given generously yourself.

Understand, the solicitor's gift needn't match what you hope the prospect will give. In fact, the amount is often less. You may be asking for $5 million, while your own stretch gift is $500. That's okay. What matters is that your giving is proportionate to your means.

Donors have every right to be suspicious if the person asking hasn't given. Why? Because the asker should care enough about the cause to be its advocate – rationally, emotionally, *and* financially.

■ Who else has given?

It's natural to want to know what peers have given. No one wants to feel she's giving away the farm, or giving too little.

Not long ago, I heard the story of a donor who each year gave $25,000 to a favorite cause. This time around, however, he was asked for $10,000 instead. When the group's newsletter appeared with a list of donors and amounts contributed, he saw that virtually all of his peers were in the $25,000 category. The fellow was outraged and embarrassed. The extra $15,000 was relatively immaterial to him. What counted more was the perception of his peers.

This story holds two lessons. One, accurate records are a must. You need to know what your donors have given. Two, by and large people want to give at the level of their peers.

One way to promote peer-level giving is to ask major donors for permission to mention their gift. Then when someone says, Who else has given? you have a ready (and inspiring) answer.

Alternatively, if you don't have a major gift to cite, you might approach your prospect this way: "We've come to you because we feel you'll understand the importance of this project. We need you to set the pattern for giving."

Lastly, if the prospect says, "I don't want to be the first big giver," you could respond by saying: "I understand how you feel. Would you consider making this a challenge gift? For example, would you agree to give $50,000 if three others do the same?"

■ Do you truly believe in this cause?

Ever notice how the best salespeople are those who genuinely believe in their product? Their enthusiasm is real – and contagious.

In the same way, a person asking for a gift must convey his own passion. He needn't be flamboyant or a skilled salesperson. But he does have to communicate his belief that this is a wonderful and worthy cause.

Even better is the solicitor who's personally touched by the cause. If, for instance, someone is approached for a gift by a cancer survivor whose life has been saved by laboratory research, it's immensely powerful.

The same would be true if the asker is a businesswoman who grew up in poverty. Then, thanks to a summer camp program funded by this organization, her life was turned around. How could you not be inspired to give?

3

"Do I Respect You?"

Let's say you're asked for $20 to help the homeless. Who would you give it to?

- Your best friend,
- Your spouse,
- An aggressive street person,
- A person who once fired you,
- Your favorite religious leader?

Most likely you would give the money to someone you trust. And you'd give willingly, maybe even enthusiastically. There's a much smaller chance you'd give to an aggressive panhandler or the boss who fired you. That's because these people have to get past your lizard brain – and that isn't easy to do.

■ Getting past your lizard brain.

Your brain has a small area on its stem called the

amygdala. It's also known as your "lizard brain" because it dictates your response to danger. It's a core survival mechanism. And because it plays a primary role in developing and storing memories of emotional events, it's much more active than we realize.

The amygdala helped humans survive for tens of thousands of years. Its function is based on pattern recognition. It told cave dwellers that a wolf could eat them, since it ate Grog. It warned them that things outside their experience are things to be wary of – from poison berries to hissing snakes.

This instinctive reaction means that a slick fundraiser will trigger memories, not of swooping pterodactyls perhaps, but of high-pressure salespeople, sleazy TV and film characters, and con artists who take advantage of unsuspecting widows.

Fortunately, it's easy to neutralize the amygdala. All you have to do is be honest and sincere (bonus: you'll feel better too). If you truly have your potential donors' interest at heart, they'll perceive it. If you don't, they'll pick that up too – and you'll never get past their threat-sensitive lizard brain.

■ How trust is earned.

Helen was hired as the foundation director of a respected hospital in a town of 60,000.

As is the case in many tight-knit communities, many of the "old guard" were unimpressed with their hospital's hiring a full-time foundation director – worse, a big-city person. Luckily Helen was sensitive to the situation.

"After three months on the job, I was invited to a Rotary luncheon by a foundation board member. Also attending was a Mr. McMillan, now in his 70s and the third generation owner of a local business. He took one look at me and whispered to his friend, 'Who's the young lady?'

"The friend explained I was the new director. And without missing a beat Mr. McMillan said, 'Director of the Foundation? What do you need her for? Raising funds for the hospital is like shooting fish in a barrel!!!'"

(Helen learned of this comment a few weeks afterward and wisecracked to her board member, "You tell Mr. McMillan to jump in that barrel and I'll give him a shot.")

Eight months later, Helen learned that Mr. McMillan had called one of the "old guard" and said he wanted to give a major gift to the hospital. He wanted his friend to set up a meeting with Helen.

"Over lunch, at his favorite restaurant, I was professional but warm," says Helen. "I listened to Mr. McMillan and tried to answer all his questions.

"Then, the real interrogation began. 'Who was I?' he asked. 'When did I get into fundraising? Why did I come to this community? What were my intentions on staying? What was happening with the Foundation? Who was serving on the board? How was I going to raise $1,000,000 for the ICU Campaign?' It was a challenge, I admit, but I answered as candidly as I could."

Helen's authenticity touched a chord. "He pulled out an envelope with a handwritten check – a big check – for the ICU project. He was a grateful patient and was motivated to give. He just wanted to make sure his gift would be managed appropriately."

But Helen didn't stop there.

She later invited McMillan to share his grateful patient story with 300 guests at the Foundation's 20th anniversary celebration. Helen introduced him by recounting the "fish in a barrel" story. The crowd knew McMillan well and enjoyed the banter. It wasn't long before Helen, with her heartfelt manner, won everyone over.

"That day when Mr. McMillan finished his story, he affirmed my position as the new foundation director and said, 'God willing, we look forward to Helen managing the administration for the next 20 years.' That sounded like a lifetime contract to me, I kidded. The crowd – 300 key community members, the core of the fundraising campaign – all laughed and applauded."

Helen's old foe had become a friend and an unwavering advocate along with the rest of the old guard.

■ Don't try this at home: threatening donors.

Helen wisely took the time to earn trust. Her instincts were good, and bore fruit. But not everyone is as patient. Some try to rush the gift, to pressure the prospect.

In his misspent youth, my friend Fraser was a leading organizer for one of Canada's political parties. For 16 years he was a part of the 'inner circle' that planned campaign strategy and advised leaders: Canada's Karl Rove, only much nicer.

Over a decade ago Fraser decided to save his soul and became a consultant to nonprofits, although he continued to support his Party with time and money.

A few years back he was contacted by a former colleague – someone he liked and trusted ... at least until the phone rang.

The Party was mounting a campaign to buy a headquarters building, the caller said, and he 'expected' Fraser to make a five-year pledge for $1,000 annually.

"His tone and his words made me feel like I was a Jersey convenience store owner," Fraser says, "and one of Tony Soprano's crew had shown up for their monthly protection payment."

Fraser continues: "When I didn't say yes right away, he played the threat and guilt cards: It would be noticed in Party circles if my name wasn't on the list, and I'd be seen as disloyal by my friends and peers."

Did the caller discuss a vision for the Party? No. Did he mention the benefits to Fraser, psychological, social, or otherwise? Apparently not. Did he convey how grateful the Party would be to receive my friend's support? Actually, the caller seemed to forget that as well.

"His pitch was chock full of assumptions, innuendo, and veiled threats," says Fraser. "As we talked, I became increasingly ticked off. Finally, I said I wasn't going to contribute. He seemed dumbfounded.

"And to further emphasize how unprofessional this fellow was, it turns out he made this call while having lunch with another campaign prospect – who overheard his end of the conversation."

It's breathtaking how many principles of good fundraising the caller violated (asking for a significant gift over the phone, violating confidentiality by having someone else in the room, using pressure tactics). But even beyond these, how did the party fundraiser go wrong? *He made it impossible for his prospect to trust him.*

You lose faith in someone who manipulates you – and you lose it instantly. Once that emotion got triggered in Fraser's lizard brain, the would-be fundraiser never had a chance.

As Buckminster Fuller said, "Integrity is the essence of everything successful."

4

"How Much Do You Want?"

Have you ever wondered, "How do I get rid of this person?"

It could be a new co-worker who drones on about his Porsche and its something or other displacement. It could be the office gossip who keeps telling you who was caught after hours with whom. Or it could be the panhandler soliciting spare change, the telemarketer, or the door-to-door salesperson.

We often want to escape from an interaction. Do our potential donors ever feel the same way about us?

Maybe. But that doesn't mean you'll lose the gift. It does mean you'll get less than you hoped for.

Decades ago when I made my first "ask" for an obscure little cause, I gathered quickly that the man I was sitting across from was less than enthusiastic to see me. I got the appointment because I could say that a prominent community member suggested I meet with him.

As I started into my well-rehearsed pitch, the man brusquely interrupted to ask his burning question:

"Will you leave my office right now if I write a check for $1,000?" That was a decent gift for the time and for this particular cause. But it was considerably less than what I had in mind.

This fellow clearly wasn't interested in the cause. And he had no reason to pander to me, a young unknown fundraiser. But I was in his office because I had invoked the name of a highly regarded personality: author and activist June Callwood.

I believe his real question to me centered around two things: "How much do you expect me to give?" and "How can I give as little as possible and still satisfy the 'obligation' to my friend?"

I admit I was taken aback by his abruptness. But I did manage a laugh and said, "Well, June Callwood said you might be able to give $5,000. Is that possible?"

I had read, no doubt like you have, that once you ask you must stop talking – immediately – and wait for the person to respond. So I simply smiled. In fact, I couldn't stop smiling.

It seemed a good hour – I bet it was no more than 60 seconds – when he finally blinked and said, "Will you leave my office if I give you $2,000?"

I told him that would be very generous. Two minutes later I had a check in hand as I rode the elevator back to reality.

■ **Be careful of what you ask for. You just might get it.**

Another friend of mine, an accomplished fundraiser, was much luckier than I ... or was she?

As the senior development officer of a large organization, she and the group's president were approaching the head of a major corporation. They had a figure in mind. But they decided to be bold – and doubled the figure. If they were successful, the gift would be one of the largest ever to their organization.

When it came time to close the deal, the president of the nonprofit steeled himself and voiced the words, "We'd like you to consider a gift of...." He was sure his pounding heart was visible through his jacket.

He didn't expect what he heard next – not by a long shot. "No problem," said the CEO, "if that's all you need, that's great. I was willing to give a lot more."

Oh my, how the solicitors wept inside. They did what all of us do from time to time: they asked for too little. In this case, seven figures too little.

Their first thought upon leaving with a check for the *very amount* they requested was: "We blew it."

So while your donor will undoubtedly think

seriously about the question: "How much do you hope I'll give?" you have to think about it even more as this example illustrates.

You would like to say "Everything you have." I advise against it. The real answer is an amount, determined in advance, that takes into account what you know about the potential donor and is based on the answers to these questions: "What is his relationship with the person or team asking?" "How skilled, well-trained, and persuasive is the person asking?" and "How clear and inspiring is your case?"

If you can accurately answer these questions, you'll find an amount that's within the prospect's giving capacity but challenges her initial assumptions on what she thought was appropriate.

■ Is Charlie more charming than me?
Short answer: Yes.

My friend Charlie used to work for a technical institute, and at its open annual meeting he heard the magic words every fundraiser longs to hear:

"I can't believe what you're doing here. I want to give."

The words were spoken to Charlie by an older man whom he'd never met. "Because I didn't know him, or what his capacity to give was, I suggested lunch a few days later. Meanwhile I discovered through research that he graduated from the school in the 1930's."

This gentleman, David was his name, had bailed hay for 13 cents a day to earn his tuition. The institute gave him a range of skills, and upon graduating he opened one profitable business after another. He was now very, very wealthy.

Over lunch, Charlie gave David and his wife an update on the school. Seeing that the couple was receptive, he said he'd develop a proposal for them.

At the follow up meeting a few weeks later, Charlie and the school's president suggested a gift to build an automotive center (an area David was clearly interested in). "We asked for $1 million and offered to name the building after him," Charlie says.

The older man paused, leaned across the table and, as though deciding upon a suit of clothes, said, "Do you have anything cheaper?" Something in the range of $100,000 to $300,000 was what he had in mind.

Sensing that David was struggling with the amount, Charlie suggested they reconnect at the end of the month. He did reiterate that the project they were offering was an ideal fit.

A few weeks later Charlie met over lunch with David and his wife. "He admitted the institute had changed his life," says Charlie. "It gave him the foundation he needed. With tears in his eyes, David said he'd give us the million dollars."

Charlie's perceptiveness – he didn't underestimate David's ability to give – and his recognition that we all need time to make a decision of the heart, were amply rewarded.

■ The first gift often leads the way.

"How much should I give?" is a question that continually runs through a donor's mind.

Some, like June Callwood's friend, want to give the least possible – but respectable – amount. They'll plumb for that level.

But even generous people will refuse sometimes, for fear of embarrassing themselves.

Take my friend, Lucinda.

She regularly contributes $1,000 to causes she knows well. But her comfort level with unfamiliar groups is $100 to $250.

Should she offer this smaller amount and be viewed as Scrooge, or is it safer to say, "Not at this time"? Unless Lucinda is made to feel that her "initial gift" is a generous gesture, she does the latter – she begs off.

Too many organizations are insensitive to people like Lucinda. Sure, you want the big gift right off, but that rarely happens. Better to view the first gift as one of many, as an overture on which to build a lasting relationship.

Capital campaign expert Kent Dove once told me that a donor's largest gift is often their 7th, 8th, or 9th gift. If there's a more powerful reason to start the giving process, I don't know it. And if doing so means welcoming $100 as you would $10,000, take comfort in the fact that philanthropists from Andrew Carnegie to Bill Gates have long used "test" gifts before committing much larger sums.

■ Overhead.

You pick up the phone: "Hi, I'm calling on behalf of the Policeman's Fund. We're raising money for...."

Beware of the word "behalf." It often means paid solicitors have been hired to raise funds. And typically, the organization that's hired them receives only a fraction of the money raised (sometimes as little as 10 percent).

You've read about these horror stories, and so have your prospects. And as a consequence, a number of them will ask: "So how much of my gift goes to overhead?"

It's both a fair and unfair question.

Fair because no one wants to give to a cause whose administrative and fundraising costs eat up 90 percent of their gift, leaving only a dime out of every dollar for the people to whom the donation is ostensibly directed.

Unfair, because many worthy grassroots and start-up groups do have higher overhead costs than giant organizations that can practice economies of scale.

So when you're asked about overhead costs, I suggest you do four things:

1) Know the numbers. What *is* your ratio of programming to overhead costs? Knowing the number might even encourage you to be more efficient.

2) Reflect back your prospect's concern. "I understand you're concerned about overhead costs. So are we. That's why we try to watch every single dollar we spend."

3) Mention a few ways you try to trim costs. Perhaps you use only donated furniture, or run a paperless office, or tap volunteer drivers, or use public facilities for your meetings. Lastly,

4) Refocus on the mission. That is, bring the conversation back to inspiring stories of the people whose lives have been changed by your organization and how the prospective donor can be a critical part of furthering this work.

To be sure, it's important to spend money wisely. But people give for emotional reasons – love, fear, anger, correcting injustice, affiliation. These are what drive major gifts, not worries about overhead costs.

5

"Why *Your* Organization?"

Mrs. Steele was called to jury duty but declined to serve, stating, "I do not believe in capital punishment."

The judge explained. "Madam, this is not a murder trial," he said. "It's simply a case in which a woman is suing her husband. He's accused of taking the $5,000 she gave him to buy a diamond necklace and donating it to charity."

"I'll serve," agreed Mrs. Steele. "I could be wrong about capital punishment."

How quickly our minds can change when we get more information.

To the question, "Why should I be interested in your particular cause?" many have a ready answer. "Because we do good work," they say. That's true, I'm sure, but many, many organizations do good work.

You need to distinguish yourself much more.

I often ask people attending my workshop to tell me their Unique Selling Proposition (USP). What is the one thing that sets their organizations apart from all the others?

Your USP could be many things: Your history, your leadership, your accomplishments, your low administrative costs, even the nature of your appeal (e.g. "Your gift of $25 will save an area of the Amazon Rainforest forever").

Dig deep enough and every organization has a distinguishing feature.

But, funny enough, in many cases your greatest asset is one you haven't thought much about, even though it's a big reason people might choose to support you.

Your stories.

When your organization is involved in helping people create art, protect the environment, support human rights, or research diseases, you create stories.

And stories can be yours alone.

- "I'm writing to you because 11 years ago the Crisis Hotline saved my daughter's life. She's now happily married and has a good job. It's because of you and other generous donors that so many desperate people in our community have someone to turn to."

• "I remember it vividly," says Dr. Ken Baum, a glaucoma specialist at Kaiser Hospital in Honolulu, Hawaii, when asked about his first Seva Mobile Eye Camp. "We were in Tibet and drove for five days to reach an older woman who was completely blind from cataracts," Ken recalls. "We did the surgery, and the next day when she took off the patch she burst into tears. She saw her grandchildren for the first time. I'll never forget that."

• "I gave up a lucrative vet practice because I saw how animals were suffering in our state and knew I had to do more. That's why I founded this organization."

People remember stories. They forget facts. Even decades later I still recall stories that motivated me to give to various causes.

This is the gift you offer to your donors – a concrete, memorable, emotional experience of helping others.

This is why *your* particular organization deserves support.

—

In their book, *Made to Stick*, Chip and Dan Heath summarize the principles that will make your cause and your stories memorable, or "sticky," as they say. They credit six key principles which they label the "Success Formula." They are:

- Simple
- Unexpected
- Concrete
- Credible
- Emotional
- Stories

Let me tell you of someone who became interested for all of the reasons above and how in turn he interested tens of thousands of people in a special cause.

John Wood was a Microsoft executive who some years ago visited the Himalayas on what is sometimes called an adventure trip. While in a Nepalese village he decided to find out what life was like for people there. And this curiosity changed his life forever.

John stopped into the local library and was shocked to find the few books there (ranging from a Danielle Steel romance novel to *Finnegan's Wake*) were so prized they were kept under lock and key.

When John later commiserated with the headmaster of the village's school, he heard something that would transform his very being. "Perhaps, sir, you will someday come back with books," said the school's head.

The following year, John did in fact return to Nepal, this time carrying 3,000 books he and his friends had donated.

And on this second visit, John decided to leave the

corporate world and devote himself entirely to building a new nonprofit. Room to Read has since created thousands of schools and libraries, provided scholarships for girls, and made a difference for millions of children in poor countries around the globe.

So why did John Wood get interested in this Nepalese village he never thought he'd see again?

First, the cause was so *simple*. He loved books and knew their value. He saw a school, a library, lots of kids, and almost no resources for them.

It was certainly *unexpected* when John asked to see the books in the library and was shown a locked container. He was quite shocked to learn that the books were kept away from the children.

John sensed he could take *concrete* action by contacting his friends and asking them to donate books that he'd personally deliver. The need was easy to quantify.

Because the campaign started with requests to his friends and contacts, it was completely *credible*; people had faith that John would uphold his promise to deliver the books. As the project turned into a nonprofit, the organization had instant credibility, too, because of John's background, his passion, and the "sacrifice" he made – giving up status and wealth to do good.

Lastly, it was *emotional* because he could tell powerful *stories* of what it meant to see these children. He could describe how important it was to give them resources to learn about life, which would dramatically improve their opportunities in the future.

In fact, John collected many of these stories in his book, *Leaving Microsoft to Change the World: An Entrepreneur's Odyssey to Educate the World's Children.*

At the 2007 Clinton Global Initiative Annual Meeting, former President Bill Clinton recognized Room to Read's work and announced the organization's commitment to double the reach of its programs by establishing 10,000 bilingual libraries by 2010. Now, that's a compelling story.

■ Deepening donors' understanding.

But you don't need epic drama to touch your donors. And good thing, since few of us could compete with John Wood's tale. A simple heartfelt conversation is still one of your mightiest tools.

Elizabeth Crook was chair of the Nashville YWCA board and she felt a desperate need to expand the Domestic Violence Shelter. The municipal government had agreed to give the YW land if the organization would double the shelter's capacity. To be successful, Elizabeth knew she'd have to reach far beyond their current donor base.

Because Nashville is a center of corporate healthcare, there are scores of wealthy entrepreneurs in the area. Elizabeth's challenge, and the key to her success, was to find a way to secure some of this "new money."

She identified as one of her potential donors a very nice fellow, close to 50, never married. On the day they met, he turned the tables on Elizabeth with his very first question. "So what about this organization interests you?" he wanted to know.

For Elizabeth that was easy. She explained how it was a cause that appealed to her heart. She felt there was a real need. And she thought the YW provided this service better than anyone.

Then Elizabeth turned to the man, "And what is near and dear to your heart?" she asked.

At first the man was caught off guard.

"Children," he replied after a long pause, "especially children who've had challenging situations at home. When I was growing up, it was the Boys and Girls Club that gave me a place to be, to feel safe. If it hadn't been for them, I don't know how my life would have turned out."

With that story in hand, it was easy for Elizabeth to focus his visit on the high percentage of women who come into the shelter with children, the quality of the YW's programs for these youngsters, and the fact that 70 percent of men in the state prison grew up in violent homes.

The man was clearly moved by the women he met and the stories he heard. He pledged $100,000, an extraordinary gift from a first-time donor. And it all happened because Elizabeth took time to find out what touched his heart and presented her cause in a way that matched his values.

Elizabeth's question to her prospect is what I would call a "killer" question. Whose heart wouldn't open and expand when asked that simple, and sincere, and disarming question: "What is near and dear to your heart?"

■ Is it interesting enough to risk going to jail?

A story can be so compelling people will even risk going to jail for it. Per Stenbeck discovered this while working at Sweden's Save the Children office.

One day the office worker who opens the mail rushed into his office, very excited.

"She held up an envelope she'd just opened and poured out its contents. Inside was $9,750 U.S. dollars in mixed denominations. There was no letter and no identification. I thanked her for her honesty (she could easily have pocketed the money) and put the cash safely away.

"On the train home I was reading the local newspaper and lo and behold I caught sight of a minor news article. The day before a bank in Stockholm had been robbed. The amount missing was $9,750. Coincidence? It couldn't be."

The next day Per contacted the police. Apparently the bills were indeed from the robbery – every single one of them.

"A week later the police caught the young thief," Per says. "It turned out he'd been so moved by a Save the Children message on television he felt he had to contribute something. Not having a penny himself, he decided to rob a bank and hand over the money to us."

There was a sad ending to this story. The man was sentenced to six months in prison and Save the Children had to return every last penny to the bank.

And what did Per learn from this experience?

"Never underestimate the pulling power of a well-orchestrated fundraising ask," he says with a wink.

6

"Will My Gift Make a Difference?"

The question, "Will my one gift make a difference?" is a core question for virtually all donors. And a closely related question is: Will my gift make a greater difference here or should I give to another cause?

As a person of modest means who loves to give, I constantly struggle with this. And I know my wealthy friends feel it acutely.

If you want ongoing support, you must show donors that they can affect a life, save an endangered animal, protect a river. It is their umbilical cord to your organization. And there are tools you can use to achieve this.

One technique is to break down the actual cost of a program and put tangible dollar amounts next to a piece of equipment, a bag of seeds, or the cost of sending a child to summer camp.

For decades Missions Across North America has run an enormously successful campaign advertising that "$2.59 will buy a meal for a homeless person." Of course, Union Gospel also gives you the option of feeding 10 people or even 100.

Another underused tool is "reporting back." Say with the help of donors your hospital raises $160,000 for a new echocardiogram machine. Some organizations mail a postcard a few days after the equipment is purchased to thank those who contributed.

Other organizations take the time to call their donors. This can be powerful, especially when you're able to tell how the donor's contribution will be used. A phone call opens up the possibility of a rich dialogue as well.

Nonprofit websites and blogs are another tool for reporting back. For a donor logging on to Greenpeace International, there are videos, petitions, photos, podcasts, games, discussion forums – all designed to involve donors (or potential donors) and to show the tremendous impact of their gifts.

A final way to show donors how their gifts matter is to arrange for them to meet with the people they help. A number of international development agencies invite major donors (who pay their own way) to visit projects in the developing world. Major environmental groups often have guided tours to spectacular wilderness areas in need of funds to protect them. On a more local level, some women's shelters invite donors to meet with the women their gifts help.

■ The best gift of all.

Dick Grace is a recovering alcoholic, retired stockbroker, and celebrated wine producer who says he's been given "the loveliest gift ... a shot at making a difference."

Dick caught the fever in 1988 while attending a wish-granting fundraiser for gravely ill children. He befriended a nine-year-old named Anthony Fraisier. Every week for six months Dick called him. And when the end came for Anthony, Dick delivered the eulogy.

Anthony's death from cancer shook Dick Grace ... but it also ignited a passion. Dick now wanted to make a difference for children. And wine would be his tool.

Since that time, Dick has raised close to $20 million for charities. And he and his wife, Ann, spend months each year visiting projects in the Himalayas where they can see firsthand the impact of their gifts.

"If you want to learn about courage, involve yourself with a cancer kid and his family," says Dick. "If you want to see resoluteness, get to know a poor Tibetan trying to eke out a living day after day for his family. If you want to see real happiness, give a simple gift like a hoop or crayons to a child in the Third World. Do this, and the joy you receive is unstoppable."

■ Smaller donors need assurance, too.

It's not unusual for major donors to be updated on the use of their contribution. But billions of dollars come from lower-dollar donors, and many of these people would give more – often much more – if you showed how their money is invested.

One South African group, the Archdiocese of Durban Zulu Missions, recently wrote to its donors sharing the story of a small group of women who started a vegetable growing project that feeds their families and turns a profit from the surplus.

The letter explained that small mechanical hoes would make the back-breaking work much easier. For donors who responded with an additional gift, the organization placed a small plaque on the hoe they'd made possible and sent back a photograph.

Responding to another appeal, a Mr. Bond from Ireland contributed funds for a wheelchair to a home for the handicapped and chronically ill. He suggested that perhaps his wheelchair could be labelled "007." In short order a plaque was installed that read "By Kind Donation of Mr Bond – 007." A picture of the wheelchair graces Mr. Bond's office.

Donors do make a fabulous difference in the world. From breakthroughs in cancer research, to schools and universities that equip people with extraordinary skills, to the environmentally endangered areas now protected forever – donors make it possible. If we tell them exactly how, they'll not only swell with pride (and rightly so) – they'll give more generously too.

7

"Is There an Urgent Reason to Give?"

Crisis. Emergency. Disaster. There's nothing more likely to raise money as fast.

Following the great Asian Tsunami, the British Disasters Emergency Committee was given a free five-minute timeslot to broadcast its appeal on all media in the UK. The result: a staggering total of more than $600 million in gifts. And it came in almost spontaneously from a British public supposedly suffering from 'donor fatigue'!

As a member of the board or staff, you may feel your cause is urgent too. After all, your income is lagging this quarter, your boss is applying pressure, the campaign chair is posing difficult questions, and time is running out.

But does that situation, as pressing as it is for you, inspire donors? In a word, no.

Michael Piraino runs a fine organization called CASA, short for Court Appointed Special Advocates. Each and every day a group of nearly 58,000 CASA volunteers advocate for abused and neglected children across the U.S. They save lives that would be otherwise lost to drugs and prison. For many kids, the situation couldn't be more urgent.

Michael told me about Dave, an entrepreneur and major donor to CASA. Dave likes CASA's work so much he wants to solicit gifts from others. He's essentially an advocate, or what Malcolm Gladwell would call a connector – someone with a broad network, and a strong desire to spread a message.

"Every time I see Dave, the first thing he says is 'Tell me a story,'" Michael tells me. "Before we get down to discussing his or anyone else's gift, Dave wants a real-life example of how we've helped a child. He wants to feel the urgency of that volunteer in the field helping a kid in need. He wants the inspiration.

"Only after he hears a story, do we move on to his questions about numbers, goals, results – all those elements that make his own business successful and which he wants to know are being used in our work."

The right kind of urgency (caring intensely) often prompts a person to exude passion – one of the most important qualities a fundraiser can have.

We may even be hard-wired this way. Our brain, science tells us, releases chemicals called opioids when we feel a sense of urgency. And these chemicals supply the energy we need to do everything from meeting deadlines, to racing around to get things done, to freeing an injured child from an otherwise immovable tree limb.

Many seem to feed off of this adrenaline rush.

■ Creating urgency.

For an organization with few or no crises, there are nevertheless ways to enhance the urgency of an appeal. For example, a school might tell the story of a student who received a scholarship, escaped poverty, became successful, and now gives back; "Think how many similar students could do the same if we had more scholarship funding. There's a student waiting for your help today."

Or take this actual case of a new agency promoting equality for people of all sexual orientations. When the group's solicitor, Kris, asked Tom and Simone for a gift of $5,000, he framed it this way:

"You and Tom are the first straight people we're approaching. We're asking you first because people know you're straight. Your support will help leverage gifts from others by showing that heterosexuals care about social justice."

Now social injustice has always been with us. So

where's the urgency here? Simply that if Tom and Simone provide the first leadership gift, others will be moved to do the same. That lends urgency. Tom and Simone can rightly feel their gift will bring in other gifts. That's inspiring.

Sometimes urgency can move donors to incredible generosity whatever their means. Mary Corkery was working for The Jesuit Centre for Social Justice during the 1980s, a time of particularly severe repression in Latin America. Six Jesuits and two women assisting the Centre were assassinated in the course of helping poor communities protect human rights. Mary wrote to her donors, urging them to help. She included a photo of one of the murdered priests.

One single mom was so moved she asked if the Jesuit Centre would accept her diamond engagement ring. It was all she had to give. Mary did her best to dissuade her, but the woman, driven to help, sent in the jewelry anyway.

■ Deadlines. Milestones. Consequences.

In the end, imparting urgency isn't terribly complicated. It can be achieved by underscoring:

A deadline: "You can send a child like Amanda to summer camp if you respond by May 31st."

A dollar amount: "Maria has the talent to attend the university. But no money. Your scholarship gift of

$18,000 will help her to achieve her dream."

The number of people recruited: "When you sign this petition you get us closer to the 20,000 people needed to convince the mayor to help the homeless."

Of course, while urgency is powerful, you'll want to use it judiciously. If you're always crying wolf, your pleas will soon be ignored.

■ **Even preparation can build a snese of urgency.**

In the mid-1990s Greenpeace was having difficulty raising funds for its campaigns to save the tropical and temperate rainforests. The forests simply didn't command the same media attention as Greenpeace's Save the Whales Campaign. Even though the need was – and remains – urgent.

At the time, Daryl Upsall was Head of Fundraising for Greenpeace International, based in Amsterdam. He knew that in Holland the Dutch Postcode Lottery distributed millions of dollars to charities. But because of internal resistance, Greenpeace had never approached the Lottery. It took Daryl a full year to persuade his colleagues to submit a request.

Greenpeace invested enormous time and effort in the presentation. "We used all the multimedia tools of the day," says Daryl, "together with in-person storytelling from colleagues who flew in from the Amazon region.

"Our presentation was stunning. We could see the Lottery management team was clearly moved. Their finance director had an almost tearful response when telling us of his childhood dream to protect the forests (he had studied and worked in this field briefly with the World Wildlife Fund). At the end he asked, 'So what is it you need?'

"We had planned for Dr. (Thilo) Bode, Executive Director of Greenpeace International, to stand up at this point and ask for a gift of $1 million."

But a combination of factors intervened.

First, Thilo saw how the presentation had created a sense of urgency among the panel members. Secondly, during their early morning preparation, Thilo and Daryl had consumed far too much, very strong, black coffee.

"It created a caffeine-induced dream," says Daryl. "We kept imagining what Greenpeace could achieve if the campaign were really well funded. As a result, we kept increasing the budget we would ask for.

"When the question came from the finance director, Thilo simply said '$10 million.' There was a gasp from the Greenpeace staff as neither of us had spoken about this to our colleagues. They were in shock, especially the senior management of Greenpeace Holland, who thought 'We were only going to ask for advice!'

"The finance director of the Lottery then answered: '$10 million – that sounds reasonable. Shall we go upstairs and sign an agreement?'"

With their exquisitely prepared presentation, Daryl and Thilo created a sense of urgency ... and then capitalized on it. They asked for, and received, ten times their initial target. That was an extra $9 million, minus $20 for espressos.

8

"Is it Easy to Give?"

Have you ever tried to donate or make a purchase online only to have the information boxes you just filled in vanish before your eyes? I have – too often. And like millions of others, I usually give up.

An email I received recently shows how it should work instead:

> I'm participating to raise money for a great cause - research to find a cure for IBD.
>
> For 13 years I personally struggled with ulcerative colitis. I was hospitalized for 180 days during that period. Eventually I was lucky enough to have surgical break-throughs help save my life. But not everyone with IBD is so lucky and that's why I'm asking you to help raise money to

find a cure!

My goal is to raise $500.00 but I can't do it without your help so please join me in raising money for a great cause by sponsoring my campaign. Just click on the link below and it will take you to my personal page where you can sponsor me.

Thank you in advance for your generosity.

Sincerely,

Mike

Now I still don't know what IBD is, and that's actually not important. There are scores of horrible diseases. But I do know Mike, who's both a colleague and a friend. So it was easy to make this decision to give. And easy to click on the link and use my credit card.

Your goal – regardless of the methods you use – should be to make giving this seamless. Over and over, we've seen that by making it easy to give, the results soar.

Once we ran an identical fundraising event twice in one night. Everything we could measure was the same – the presentation, the audience size, the pitch. But at one event, people could use cash only. At the other, people could write a check.

We raised 10 times the amount when donors could give by check – something audience composition was unlikely to account for – and we also collected donor names and addresses.

Both checks and credit cards made it easier to give *and* prompted individuals to think in amounts much greater than what they'd normally drop into a basket.

■ **For want of a stamp.**

In 1981 an organization I truly respect sent me an appeal. I wrote a check and put it in their reply envelope. Then it sat on my counter for four weeks.

Why? Because I didn't/couldn't get around to buying a stamp. It was inconvenient, a bother, and the organization hadn't provided a paid return envelope. Four weeks later, the emotion generated by an inspirational letter had faded. I still remember thinking: Well, my credit union account IS overdrawn, I'll make a gift later.

Later turned into 25 years! This group (to which I do now give) almost certainly lost 25 years of gifts because they didn't make it convenient for me to give.

■ **My favorite easy giving method.**

Many billions of dollars of "convenient" gifts are raised each month by charities around the world. Donors simply make a monthly pledge (once!) and thereafter money is automatically transferred from their bank account or credit card to the organization(s) of their choice.

While it goes by different names – Electronic Funds

Transfer, pre-authorized checking, direct debit – monthly giving represents a true growth area at a time when (outside of major gifts) nonprofits are often treading water.

Best of all, it retains more donors than any other giving method – usually 80 to 95 percent annually depending on the method of recruitment and how donors are treated.

Contrast that with the 35 to 50 percent of new direct mail donors who give again; or the 5 to 40 percent of special event donors; or the 10 to 40 percent of telethon donors. You can see the advantage of monthly giving.

Amnesty International has tens of thousands of monthly donors. When AI asked why they use this method, a total of nine percent of the monthly donors said it was because the organization works to stop torture. That was the second highest reason. The primary reason – at an astounding 52 percent - was because monthly giving is convenient.

I am currently on six monthly plans. As I write this I've been giving for 3 years, 4 years, 9 years, 17 years, 19 years, and 30 years. A decade from now that almost certainly will read: Giving for: 13 years, 14 years, 19 years, 27 years, 29 years, 40 years. Add it all up and that's a total of 1,420 gifts (not counting the extra checks I send from time to time). And, not surprisingly, a few of these causes are in my will.

I bring this up not to boast of my generosity, but to show that once a donor like me comes aboard, inertia takes over. I recall one of these causes did something to irritate me so I decided to reduce my monthly gift. That was 12 years ago! I never got around to it. I can't even remember now why I was so peeved.

■ Shall we explore the possibilities?

Most people don't hide their assets under a mattress. In fact, much of the world's wealth is tied up in securities, real estate, and private companies. Essentially your donors and prospects don't have much sitting in a cash account ready to give to you.

That's why creative thinking and "making it easy" are key tools for an effective fundraiser.

My colleague Jimmie Alford, mentioned before in these pages, once identified a million-dollar prospect. But there was a problem, admittedly a big one. The prospect made it clear he could only give $100,000 – no more.

Now Jimmie is focused on relationships and transformational gifts, and rather than confirm the $100,000 commitment, he sensed the prospect's desire to give more. So Jimmie posed the simple but brilliant question to him: Would you be willing to explore how you might be able to give more?

Voila! Through the process of building trust and exploring different ways of giving, the individual decided to transfer a piece of property valued at $975,000. Coupled with his initial $100,000 check, the organization received more than 10 times the original gift offer.

■ Ease is part of please.

Does your organization devote countless hours to identifying donors, researching their giving capacity, training just the right volunteer to solicit, and developing letter perfect proposals? Funny how little this all means if you fail to remember to do one simple thing – make it easy for the donor to give.

I'll illustrate the point I'm making with a vignette about my wife, Marcia.

The other night, she and I were in bed reading. Marcia was at a turning point in her book and asked if I'd mind getting her a glass of water. No problem. I'm a sensitive west coast kind of guy (and besides I had to get up and use the facility).

As I was trotting down the stairs Marcia asked – since I was up anyway now – if I wouldn't mind turning out the bathroom light ... and checking on the kids ... and turning on the dishwasher ... and letting the dog out one last time.

By the time I got back, I had forgotten my wife's glass of water. And I wasn't about to go back for it.

Remember if you make things too complicated you may not get what you were really looking for.

9

"How Will I Be Treated?"

For some donors this can mean, Will I be acknowledged? How will I be recognized? Or even, Will you forget about me once I give?

A friend of mine, a major donor to many good causes, has the simplest of requests.

"My only concern is how easy it'll be to get a tax receipt," she says. "It is totally frustrating not to receive the receipt and have to chase it down. When this happens, I won't give to that group again."

You'd think that efficiently sending a thank-you and a receipt would be as routine as brushing your teeth every morning. Yet for many groups it isn't.

Over the years I've tested the recognition systems of many organizations in the U.S. and Canada. And what

I've discovered is discouraging. Once we sent gifts to 28 hospitals, and received only a few warm thank-yous in return – some of them taking weeks to arrive. One hospital took more than three months to respond. Appalling? Yes. Rare? Hardly.

And if you think it's hard getting your gift acknowledged, it's worse trying to initiate a gift. I contacted 100 organizations asking how I could join their monthly giving program. Nearly half didn't respond even though many of the non-responders did in fact have such a program. Imagine that. Fifty organizations ignored my overture to give!

Another study I ran on legacy programs produced similar results: I received no response from about half of the groups I contacted. And that's after I expressed a *specific interest* in leaving a bequest.

■ What's your attitude?

Kristin Castle would never neglect a donor that way. She's what I call an ideal database manager. "I hate it when once we've got their money, we don't care about them anymore," she says of her donors. "So in my own little way, I try to be that one person who cares." Kristin, who works in New Zealand, is a living example of why hiring for "attitude" is a great strategy.

Years ago when she was working at a women's shelter, a Mr. Smith wrote a short letter of apology to the organization. It turns out his wife of 50-odd years had recently died. He was now on a single pension and could no longer afford to give.

"I wrote back," says Kristin, "saying how sorry and saddened we were that his wife had died and how much we appreciated their support over the years. And we understood it was no longer possible for him to give, but assured him how much the donations he and his wife made had made a difference.

"A couple of weeks later Mr. Smith wrote again. In his second letter, he explained that he and his wife had supported approximately 30 charities over their lifetime. He had written to every one of them explaining his changed circumstances. Amazingly, only three wrote back. Even more astonishingly, out of those three only one (us) said 'sorry' (for his bereavement)."

Because of Kristin's kindness, Mr. Smith pledged to continue to support the shelter with as much as he could afford. "I know he gave what he could with all his heart, and I know how hard it must have been for him to write those 30 letters, 30 times putting in writing that his beloved wife had died after a long and happy marriage."

Will Mr. Smith leave a legacy? Who can say? But what I do know is that out of a hundred donors who receive this level of care, this respect, this appreciation, a few will be motivated to do so. And as importantly, most will tell their friends just how wonderful your organization is.

■ One donor's fear.

Some donors never want to hear from you again. Most donors do.

When he was in his early 30s and "just a kid," Tom Wilson was the campaign director for a U.S. hospital. As part of the organization's legacy giving effort, Tom met regularly with a widow in her late 70s. She lived in a nearby retirement community.

"The woman expressed interest in the hospital and was encouraging about the potential for a charitable unitrust in the mid six-figures range," Tom says. "We kept meeting and meeting but I couldn't close the gift. After about the eighth session (me being slow), I told her we needed to resolve things either way, positive or negative – otherwise my bosses wouldn't let me keep visiting."

Here's what she said:

"Oh, I guess I'd better make the gift then. But, will you still visit with me? I'm so lonely. I didn't really want to string you along, but I was afraid once I gave you wouldn't see me again. I hate to lose our relationship."

Now Tom is charming, witty, and good looking (according to some), so you can understand her position. But she's not alone. Many donors fear abandonment – often with good reason.

Too many donors are forgotten once they make the big gift. It may be because of staff turnover, poor recordkeeping, or seeing the gift as a final transaction (rather than the start of an enduring relationship). The list is long, the behavior inexcusable.

The irony is that these donors are always the best prospects for the next campaign. Givers tend to give again. It's a habit they develop. But waiting to reconnect before the next ask is both bad fundraising and bad manners.

So, how did Tom handle his donor's fear?

"I assured her of the stewardship function of fundraisers. We don't just raise money, we attend to all of our donors of record. So of course I would be back at least yearly. If she wanted to see me more often, she needed to help me raise more money."

Tom then brilliantly asked if she could host "teas" for her friends to tell them why she had converted her long-term stock to a charitable unitrust. She thought this was a great idea. "Once a year was okay, but once a month was even better," was how she put it.

Tom's sensitivity and kindness led to millions in gifts for his hospital.

■ Other ways to recognize.

I've cited specific cases here of people and organizations that took the time to recognize their donors. But let's quickly explore some general ways you can increase the connection your donors feel.

Among the best (assuming it's appropriate for your

cause) are site tours. There's nothing more powerful than letting donors see the work you do with their own eyes.

Occasional phone calls from organizational leaders simply to thank donors – and not to ask for a gift – are both surprising and memorable.

Clipping a newspaper article, either about your organization or related to your mission, and sending it to a donor can be effective – especially if you include a post-it note giving the donor credit for making this possible.

Along similar lines, Tim Sanders in his fine book, *Love Is The Killer App*, suggests sending special people – perhaps your very top donors – an appropriate book or CD.

Lastly, you might follow consultant Terry Axelrod's advice. She encourages organizations to invite multi-year donors to special events, making sure they leave with the feeling, "I'm glad I give money here. Maybe I could give more."

■ It matters more than you think.

A number of years ago I was visiting with a woman in New York, a major donor to many causes. We were talking about philanthropy in general, and after dinner she invited me into her study. There, she pulled out a file of correspondence she'd received from various organizations.

Some of it was years old. She showed me dog-eared annual reports in which she and her late husband were listed as donors. She brought out thank-you letters and read from a few of them fondly. There were even invitations to events she treasured to this day.

It was clear to me how she relished these things. For her, recognition was no empty gesture.

10

"Will I Have a Say Over How You Use My Gift?"

Parents know they don't have a lot of control ...

When your infant demands a feeding at two in the morning.

When your teen listens to gangster rap despite your distaste.

When your cum laude angel becomes engaged to a ne'er-do-well.

You can quickly start to feel powerless. But you can still hope to have "influence."

And that's what many donors want – and deserve ... as long as it stops there.

Ray Rasker lives in Montana, a long way from most

major donors. So he was delighted when a young Silicon Valley entrepreneur moved to Bozeman. More delighted, because the fellow telephoned to say he wanted to give a substantial gift to the environmental organization where Ray worked.

Now for the most part, "unknown" multi-millionaires aren't ringing up nonprofits. But, like many delightful opportunities, this one came with strings. In exchange for his gift, the man wanted a seat on the board. But more importantly he wanted to change the organization's mission.

Says Ray: "He called himself a 'venture philanthropist,' so the rules, at least from his perspective, were different. Just as a venture capitalist wants some degree of control over the business he invests in, this man felt he could translate the same thinking to the nonprofit world."

In this case, Ray's would-be donor wanted more than control over his gift. He wanted control of the organization. Ray of course demurred. "That didn't fit for us," he politely phrases it.

■ Regaining control.

My friend Daryl had a similar problem. But the potential gift he was offered was vastly greater. There was only one problem. The donors wanted to spend it on something that wasn't needed.

Freddie Mercury, the lead singer of Queen, died in

1991 from AIDS. At the time, Daryl was Head of Fundraising for the Terrence Higgins Trust, one of the largest HIV/AIDS charities in the world.

The manager of Queen called and asked Daryl for a meeting. The band wanted to release "Bohemian Rhapsody" and direct all royalties and profits to the Terrance Higgins Trust, so long as the money would build the "Freddie Mercury HIV/AIDS Ward" in a hospital.

Daryl's dilemma was that the UK didn't need such a ward. By then, anti-retroviral drugs had been introduced, improving the health and life expectancy of those with HIV and leading to an oversupply of beds. Plus, the medical profession was no longer isolating HIV/AIDS patients in hospitals.

What were Daryl's choices? He could take the money, with the perk of singing backup at the tribute concert. Or he could use his skills to negotiate a different arrangement (a better choice, since he can't carry a tune).

After two meetings, and long hours of negotiation, Daryl finally persuaded Queen, its management team, and their record company to accept his view – they should use the money to advocate for those with HIV/AIDS and to launch a campaign to prevent its transmission.

The parties ceded control because Daryl listened to them, understood their viewpoint, and showed them how the funds could have greater impact. "Bohemian Rhapsody" went straight to number one in the UK and many places worldwide. The record raised a total of $10 million.

■ What has changed?

Why is it that donors want more control these days? I think it's for a couple of key reasons.

1) They don't trust you'll spend their money wisely
2) They feel more involved when they have control

Let's deal with each briefly.

First, trust. In our society, we've seen a decline of trust for virtually all institutions and authorities. And this includes nonprofits. No doubt the media is partly to blame.

I suspect that on a per capita basis there are fewer ethical transgressions today than at any point in the last 100 years. There are more checks and balances, more transparency, and a greater willingness to expose wrongdoing. But the occasional scandal, given great airplay (a good thing actually), does periodically undermine trust in the charitable sector.

As to the second reason, that donors feel more involved when they have control, perhaps it's nothing more than a simple yearning for human contact. Think of the ways we increasingly isolate ourselves. For instance, why meet with someone or call a friend when you can catch up by email?

A donor saying, "I want to see how you put my gift to work" may not be interested in heavy-handed control at all.

Rather, he may simply want to see the child who will get a new wheelchair. Or he may want to meet the refugees learning English in a class he helped to make possible. That strengthens the emotional link, and the feeling that he's helped change lives.

For the fundraiser, this is always an opportunity.

■ Getting your answers straight.

So let me pose a question to you.

What answer can you give when a major donor asks: what influence will I have over my gift?

You may have one answer. Your boss or board may have another, or even offer a variety of conflicting answers.

That won't inspire confidence.

Clarifying in advance, and in writing, what "control" you're willing to give donors will mean that when a wealthy young entrepreneur, a world-famous rock band, or any other donor offers you a gift with strings, you'll be able to take advantage of the opportunity without trading away your organization's soul.

Or your own.

■ One last dilemma.

So what happens if that new exhibition hall you were going to build, and name after the donor whose juicy gift made it possible, is no longer feasible? What do you do with the gift? What do you tell the donor?

First off, you call and tell her the truth. Then you offer to return the gift, if appropriate. Almost certainly this will build trust and enhance your reputation and ability to acquire future gifts. And many donors will so much respect your integrity they'll tell you to keep the gift.

During the 2005 Tsunami crisis, several major charities ranging from the American Red Cross to OXFAM ceased raising reconstruction funds when they hit their spending targets.

Doctors Without Borders returned more than $500,000 it couldn't use. "We didn't want the restricted funds to outpace our capacity to use them effectively in the field," said Nicolas de Torrento, the organization's executive director.

This is responsible fundraising. Moreover it adds to your reputation as an organization that cares how donor dollars are used and it builds loyalty among your supporters.

For an example of irresponsible fundraising, look no further than MADD Canada, which counted tens of millions of dollars in telemarketing expenses as a mission-related charitable activity.

A newspaper exposé forced a public apology and a board commitment to transparency. Time will tell what the impact will be, but MADD will certainly be scrutinized closely in the future. In time, with proper accounting and expenditures, the organization may recover its credibility. But it won't be anytime soon.

11

"How Will You Measure Results?"

Mike Bartlett was in the middle of his pitch to a local corporate leader. Knowing the man had an eye for numbers, Mike launched into a review of the media impressions, customer touch-points, and other value-added elements this partnership with his nonprofit would generate for the corporation.

"After – quite frankly – rambling for 30 seconds or so, he stopped me," Mike says.

"No," the man interrupted. "What I'm asking is how will you measure whether my contribution will benefit the hospital?"

Others might have been flustered, but not Mike. In fact, he was delighted by the question. It showed the prospect had an interest in making a gift. And, it demonstrated that he cared how his company's money would be used (if it were used properly, more gifts might be forthcoming).

Like most good fundraisers, Mike was prepared with his answer. Down to the dollar, he was able to cite the hospital's urgent equipment needs. More importantly he was able to link those needs with how they would help individual patients ("A gift of $28,200 would buy a transfusion device that saves lives by getting blood into patients six times faster than a regular IV drip").

Oh sure, some donors – especially corporate – key in on the benefits to *them*. But even these people want to know how your cause makes a difference in the community and in the lives of others.

■ Do donors really care about measurement?

An article by Katie Cunningham and Marc Ricks in the summer 2004 issue of *The Stanford Social Innovation Review* interviewed donors about measurement. Out of the 22 donors – each of whom had given more than $50,000 annually – four were keenly interested in receiving more information about the organization's performance.

Given the small sample size, this isn't statistically significant. But it does suggest that some generous donors do worry about results, and that portion may be growing. Younger wealthy donors seem to desire more measurement. Better to err on the side of more feedback than less – unless your donors tell you otherwise.

That doesn't mean you have to produce complex, detailed reports, however. Material that's quick, data-driven, and emotional will still keep gifts coming from those who genuinely care about measurement.

Recently I was at a fundraising event with John Wood, founder of Room to Read, whom I spoke about earlier. He's a man whose measurement of results, strategic goals, and business savvy have raised tens of millions of dollars.

John's presentation was a fine example of good storytelling, strong visuals, and hard figures. He cited the number of schools built, number of libraries, books printed, scholarships offered. He showed the scale of growth (faster than Starbucks), and his business audience was clearly impressed.

John went on to tell his personal story: how he abandoned his high-paying Microsoft job once he was exposed to the needs of children in Nepal. He inspired us by telling of how communities came together to build libraries and schools for their children. And of course he introduced us to a number of individual kids whose lives will be changed forever by the gift of literacy.

While John was exquisitely prepared, he didn't present a lengthy detail-laden report on Room to Read.

Instead he delivered highlights substantiated by numbers. Just enough, but not too much, to satisfy those who take measurements to heart.

■ So how do you measure results?

The answer depends on your sector; obviously some groups have a more difficult time than others.

Room to Read has it easy in some ways. It can say such things as: "$2,500 builds a library" or "$250 gives a child a school scholarship for a year." On the other hand, an environmental advocacy group trying to stop a mine from polluting a river has a more difficult time.

And yet, if they try, every group can calculate the value of what a gift can do.

Say an environmental group needs $25,000 for its anti-pollution campaign. If it costs $1 for each contact, then a gift of $50 would reach 50 families. That's 50 families who would know more about what's at stake for the future of their community's river.

Or $120 could pay for a day's salary of a campaigner to go door to door to raise awareness. You get the picture. With the magic of fifth grade math, you divide, multiply, and calculate dollar tags for each component of the work you do.

There are two measurement tools donors like:

- Numbers
- Stories

Measurement through numbers.

A certain kind of donor likes hard numbers. Often the bigger the better.

• "Your community hospital serves 600 emergency patients a day – more than any other hospital in the city."

• "Your contribution helped us serve 1,756 meals to the poor on Thanksgiving."

• "$100,000 can provide scholarships to 10 deserving students who couldn't otherwise afford to attend the university."

Each of these examples is the start of measurement. The extension of this would be to report more detail:

• "There was an average of three heart attack victims rushed to the Emergency Room every day. We were able to save 1,095 lives last year. Imagine how many family members are grateful that you donated $____."

• "The 1756 meals included feeding 72 children whose parents have fallen on hard times."

• "19 out of 20 scholarship students graduated. 13 went on to get second degrees including 4 Master's Degrees, 1 in law, 1 in engineering, 1 MBA, 2 in medicine, and 1 Ph.D."

Here, you're detailing exactly how the donor's gift

transformed lives and contributed significantly to the community.

Measurement through stories

Stories can incorporate a discussion of numbers, but they can also stand on their own. And if you had to choose one or the other you should always choose the story.

"How do we measure your gift's impact? Let me tell you the story of my baby.

"When our baby Jack was born, it was the first time I saw my husband cry. I remember lying on the delivery bed listening to the emergency call for the respiratory therapist, hearing the urgency in the voices of my nurses and doctor.

"We'd known, even before the decision to deliver Jack seven weeks early, that there was something seriously wrong with him.

"Jack was born with a rare condition called an omphalocele. He was born with his liver, stomach and intestines in a sac outside his body, attached to his umbilical cord.

"The nurses told us to prepare ourselves – to prepare for the worst. But thanks to the amazing expertise and loving care provided by the doctors and nurses at the hospital – and Jack's fighting spirit – we were finally able to take our baby home for good, nine long months later, just before the holidays.

"Our gratitude at being able to celebrate the holidays together as a family with Jack's 3-year old brother, Tommy, was overwhelming. I find it hard to express the debt I feel we owe to this great hospital and their incredible staff. They saved my baby!

"Which is why I'm writing to you today – to sincerely thank you for your past support of the hospital. You helped provide the world-class medical staff, technology, and equipment that enabled Jack to survive."

Stories are almost always more powerful than numbers. And yet you have to be prepared with both for two reasons: one to prove you track these things and two because some donors really do want to know.

■ When a donor asks, it's another gift.

Robert Frost said, "Wood chopped warms you twice." In a similar way, your being asked, "How will you measure results?" is actually a donor's second gift to you.

The question forces you to develop evaluation criteria, often leading to a more effective allocation of your resources, and a streamlined organization. Further, when a donor poses this question, take it as a good sign. It usually means she's ready to give, but wants to be sure she's giving wisely.

TWO-MINUTE REVIEW

To help you prepare for your visits with donors, here's a quick summary of the core questions we've discussed in this book:

Why me?

If you remember that "me" is everyone's favorite subject, it will help train your focus where it should be: on the prospect and how his or her gift will make a difference in the world.

Why are *you* asking me?

For each donor, Why are you asking me? essentially means: What's in it for you? and Have you given yourself? and just what are your motives? If you have genuine passion for the cause, it'll show through, lending comfort to the donor and credibility to your ask.

Do I respect you?

There's no more critical trait for a fundraiser than integrity. When people trust you, they're open to what you have to say. But trust takes time. You can't rush it. You earn respect by showing that you genuinely care about the prospect and the cause.

How much do you want?

Most donors want to give what they perceive as fair –

not too much, not too little. It takes legwork, and perhaps a conversation with someone who knows the prospect, but you need to arrive at a dollar figure that challenges but is nevertheless seen as realistic by the donor.

Why *your* organization?

We all know there are thousands of wonderful causes. So how do you make yours stand out? The key is your stories. What makes you unique and different from every other organization are the stories you tell about the people you help.

Will my gift make a difference?

Your goal as a fundraiser is to show donors, in practical, tangible ways, how their financial support will change and improve the life of a fellow human being, or a dog and cat, or protect an environmental treasure. If you don't show this, your prospect will give to another cause where he can see a positive impact.

Is there an urgent reason to give?

While you can't manufacture it, there is some urgency for most organizations: the faster the gift comes in, the sooner you can aid the people needing help. Deadlines, targets, and emotional stories are all your friends in this regard.

Is it easy to give?

As a fundraiser, you continually want to look for ways to make it easy for donors to give. That could be the convenience of using a credit card, a toll-free number, having easy to fill out forms, or, my personal favorite, a monthly giving program.

How will I be treated?

Part of treating donors well is showing kindness at all giving levels. From placing their names on plaques, to site visits, to properly thanking donors, there are many ways to treat donors with consideration and respect. When you do, the gifts will keep on coming.

Will I have a say over how you use my gift?

While some donors want control, most will trust your organization to spend their gift wisely ... IF you've first listened to, heard, and have fully appreciated any concerns they have in this regard.

How will you measure results?

A certain percentage of donors, especially major givers, want measurable results. So in addition to having memorable stories to tell, as a solicitor you must know the numbers too. How many people you serve, how much money buys a certain piece of equipment, the number of people who have successfully passed through your program – all of these serve to reassure the donor that she's made a wise investment in you.

POSTSCRIPT

Throughout this book I've shared some stories from a wide variety of talented fundraisers. In their careers, these seasoned experts have made lots of mistakes. That's what "seasoned" means. But something kept driving them on.

Today they happily earn a good living *and* make the world a better place. I personally can't think of anything I'd rather do than raise money for great causes. I hope you feel the same way.

Whether you serve on the board, or at the board's pleasure, you have a vital role in society. You connect generous people with causes that matter. You help build a legacy that will continue serving your mission long after you're gone. And your good work will help many people you'll never meet.

• The child who receives a scholarship and goes on to discover a miracle cure.

• The team of volunteer activists who save an

endangered forest – helping to preserve a place where your great-grandchildren will traipse one day.

• Or perhaps you raise funds to build an arts center that will bring the joy of good theatre to your community long into the future.

I've tried to show you some of what we've learned about a donor's mind – the patterns you can expect.

Whether spoken or not, you can be sure donors will ask these 11 questions. I know that from experience. But then so do you. Because they're the very same questions *you* have when you're approached for a gift.

I'll be honored if you heed my advice. But more important – listen to your own heart. It's there where you'll find the very answers you, and your donors, crave.

ACKNOWLEDGMENTS

Last year, Jerry Cianciolo, editor of Emerson & Church, Publishers, approached me to write a book on the questions donors usually ask. I thought, That's a great idea. So thank you Jerry for the opportunity and for your tight editing.

This book is possible because of the great work of many fundraisers. First I'd like to thank the people who sent me wonderful stories that we simply did not have room enough for (although you may see them in another book someday!). And also thanks to the people whose stories we did use:

Iain Simpson, Fraser Green, Julie Weston, Helen DeBoer, Ross Marsh, John Wood, Kitty Hilton, Karen Van Sacker, Terry Axelrod, Elizabeth Crook, Per Stenbeck, Martha Kowalick, Pierre-Bernard Le Bas, Michael Piraino, Mary Corkery, Daryl Upsall, Jeanie Magee, Kirstin Castle, Dick Grace, Ray Rasker, Mike Bartlett, Simone Joyeaux, Terry Murray, Allan Arlett.

In addition I'd like to especially thank Mal Warwick, Tom Ahern, Jerry Panas, Ken Burnett,

Nick Allen, Andy Robinson, Tom Wilson, and Jimmie Alford for your insightful comments on the manuscript and all the wonderful work you do for the profession, as trainers, fundraisers, and inspiring leaders.

I'm also grateful to my staff members who helped with this book: Carla Voss, Trisha Hubbard, Lynne Boardman, and Jennifer Hargreaves. Our designers, Elaine Donovan and Glenn Gaetz did a superb job designing the cover. And special thanks go to Dorothy Bartoszewski for her highly useful comments, editing, and good humor.

And without the many generous donors I have met, and the many great clients Harvey McKinnon Associates has worked with, I would not have my own stories to contribute to this book – so a special thanks to all of you.

Lastly, I want to thank my wife Marcia, and my sons James and Ian who ask a lot of questions of their own, such as "When are you going to finish this book?" or "Do we have to go to bed now?" They have helped me think about answers to important questions.

ABOUT THE AUTHOR

Harvey McKinnon is co-author of the international bestseller, *The Power of Giving* (Tarcher/Penguin), selected as an Amazon Best Book for 2005. His other works include, *Hidden Gold*, and the audio CD *How Today's Rich Give* (Jossey-Bass), as well as the *Tiny Essentials of Monthly Committed Giving* (White Lion Press).

McKinnon, who is one of North America's leading fundraising experts, runs the Vancouver/Toronto based fundraising consultancy, Harvey McKinnon Associates (HMA).

HMA works with clients in many countries, ranging from children's causes to environmental groups to hospitals. McKinnon has served on many boards over the years and lives with his family in Vancouver, Canada.

Also by Harvey McKinnon

THE POWER OF GIVING

Giving does more than improve the lives of others – it affects our own lives profoundly, with benefits ranging from the practical, such as improved health and professional connections, to the intangible, like hope and a sense of connection with others.

A great book for fundraisers, and volunteers, *The Power of Giving* shows you how the act of giving fulfills a fundamental human need. It is a must-read for anyone interested in improving the world – and their own lives in the process.

"We've needed a book like this for a long time. Now it's your turn to help. Buy it, share it, give a copy to a friend. This book could change everything."
   — **Seth Godin**, Author of *Purple Cow*

"This powerful and inspiring book will help you live a more significant life and become more the person that you were meant to be."
   — **Robin Sharma**, Author of *The Monk Who Sold His Ferrari*

"Extremely impressive ... very inspiring."
   — **Dr. Wayne Dyer**, Author of *The Power of Intention*

"If everyone followed the advice given in this wonderful book, our world would be a richer, more equitable, and peaceful place."
   — **Jack Canfield**, Co-creator of the *Chicken Soup for the Soul* series

Published by Penguin Group (USA)

INDEX

The Gold Standard in Books for Your Board

Read each in an hour • Quantity discounts up to 50 percent

The Ultimate Board Member's Book
Kay Sprinkel Grace, 114 pp., $24.95, ISBN 1889102180

Here is a book for *all* nonprofit boards: those wanting to operate with maximum effectiveness, those needing to clarify exactly what their job is, and those wanting to ensure that all members are 'on the same page.' It's all here in jargon-free language: how boards work, what the job entails, the time commitment, fundraising responsibilities, and much more.

How Are We Doing?
Gayle L. Gifford, 120 pp., $24.95, ISBN 1889102237

Until now, almost all books dealing with board evaluation have had an air of unreality about them. The perplexing graphs, the matrix boxes, the overlong questionnaires. Enter Gayle Gifford, who has pioneered an elegantly simple way for your board to evaluate and improve its overall performance. It all comes down to answering a host of simple, straightforward questions.

The Fundraising Habits of Supremely Successful Boards
Jerold Panas, 108 pp., $24.95, ISBN 1889102261

Jerold Panas has observed more boards at work than perhaps anyone in America, all the while helping them to surpass their campaign goals of $100,000 to $100 million. *Fundraising Habits* is the brilliant culmination of what Panas has learned firsthand about boards who excel at the task of resource development.

Big Gifts for Small Groups
Andy Robinson, 104 pp., $24.95, ISBN 1889102210

If yours is among the tens of thousands of organizations for whom six- and seven-figure gifts are unattainable, then this book is for you and your board. You'll learn everything you need to know: how to get ready for the campaign, whom to approach, where to find them, where to conduct the solicitation, what to bring with you, how to ask, how to make it easy for the donor to give, and what to do once you have the commitment.

Fundraising Mistakes that Bedevil All Boards (and Staff Too)
Kay Sprinkel Grace, 109 pp., $24.95, ISBN 1889102229

Fundraising mistakes are a thing of the past. Or, rather, there's no excuse for making a mistake anymore. If you blunder from now on, it's simply evidence you haven't read Kay Sprinkel Grace's book, in which she exposes *all* of the costly errors – 40 in total – that thwart us time and again.

Emerson & Church, Publishers
www.emersonandchurch.com

Copies of this and other books from the
publisher are available at discount when
purchased in quantity for boards of directors
or staff. Call 508-359-0019 or visit
www.emersonandchurch.com